About the Creators of This Calendar

Dawn Huffaker is an established poet who has written for more than 25 years. She primarily writes about the incredible beauty in nature. Her goal is to paint a memorable picture with her words. This is her fifth calendar. So far, she has published two books of poetry available at Amazon. Learn more about her at www.dawnhuffaker.com

Dawn is unable to walk. She lives her life from a motorized wheelchair. Doing photography is quite difficult for her. She focuses on her poetry, instead.

Since she is unable to take her own photos, Dawn has been blessed with a family that is very talented with a camera. This year, the calendar includes beautiful nature photography from her parents, Marilyn & Ron Huffaker, and her sister, Chris Knight. They each add much to Dawn's poetry.

I0435311

Cold January

Snowflakes tumble from the sky.
Juncos seek sustenance
From the feeder found here.
Crack, crunch, crush, repeat.
Seed squabbles settled quickly-
Hop, fly, or chase, it doesn't matter.

Cold January has arrived.
Snow stacks on surfaces white
Like feathers from a fluffy down pillow.
Trees sway slower.
Ground muffled mute.
Time to rest and reflect.

December's excitement is over.
New year is recuperating from it.
Plans are pondered by one and all.
Resolutions broken by noon. Darn!
Life moves on at a gentle crawl.
Meditate on the snow as it
Falls, falls, falls.

- Dawn L. Huffaker

Photo by Marilyn Huffaker

January 2015

Sunday	Monday	Tuesday	Wednesday	Thursday	Friday	Saturday
				1 New Year's Day	2	3
4 ○	5	6	7	8	9	10
11	12	13 ◐	14	15	16	17
18	19 Martin Luther King Day	20 ●	21	22	23	24
25	26 ◑	27	28	29	30	31

Photo by Marilyn Huffaker

Blushing, Baby Blossoms

Blushing, baby blossoms
Slowly open skyward.
Sun shines softly on satin petals
Newly exposed to all.

This gentle glow graces
Their upturned faces.
What promise there is
In each blossom's eager smile!

Bees bounce by
Performing pirouettes and pas de deux,
As they pollinate the blossoms
To prepare them for motherhood.

An ancient dance has begun anew.
Sun shares shimmering rays.
Bees dance their best ballet.
Blossoms happily bob in place.

Spring is on her way...

– Dawn L. Huffaker

February 2015

Sunday	Monday	Tuesday	Wednesday	Thursday	Friday	Saturday
25	26	27	28	29	30	31
1	2	3 ○	4	5	6	7
8	9	10	11 ◑	12 Lincoln's Birthday	13	14 Valentine's Day
15	16 Washington's Birthday	17	18 ●	19	20	21
22	23	24	25 ◐	26	27	28

Infant Season

Tulips taste the soft, washed air.
Delighting in the delicate flavor.
Excited about the infant season.
All is fresh. All is new.
How will this spring unfold?

Buds begin unfurling-
Whispering wistfully of
Wants and whims.
Breeze brushes by.
Cold air cycles through.

Sunshine showers them with warmth.
Cheery, swirled tulips open to the sky.
Leaves stretch out in loving homage.
Gray winter has been dethroned; defeated.
Budding baby spring begins her reign today.

- Dawn L. Huffaker

Photo by Marilyn Huffaker

March 2015

Sunday	Monday	Tuesday	Wednesday	Thursday	Friday	Saturday
1	2	3	4	○ 5	6	7
8 Daylight savings time begins	9	10	11	12	◑ 13	14
15	16	17 St. Patrick's Day	18	19	● 20 Vernal Equinox 22:45 UTC	21
22	23	24	25	26	◐ 27	28
29	30	31				

Miss Iris

Miss Iris stirred from her slumber
One warm, April morn.
With a yawn and a stretch,
She swept the mental cobwebs away.
Today was important.
No time to waste. Spring was calling.

Testing the dirt above her,
Miss Iris unfurled her infant leaves.
They wiggled and wove their way beyond.
Gentle sun greeted their new arrival
With welcome warmth and a tender touch.
She gratefully felt his loving presence.

Kind days coaxed her to grow.
Leaves made food with great abandon.
Miss Iris was soon ready to bloom.
Majestic bud rose high for proud display.
Passionate, purple petals unwrapped to adorn her.
Sun's kiss was given in approval.

– Dawn L. Huffaker

April 2015

Sunday	Monday	Tuesday	Wednesday	Thursday	Friday	Saturday
29	30	31	1	2	3	4
					Good Friday	
5	6	7	8	9	10	11
Easter						
12	13	14	15	16	17	18
19	20	21	22	23	24	25
			Earth Day			
26	27	28	29	30	1	2

March 2015

Su	Mo	Tu	We	Th	Fr	Sa
1	2	3	4	5	6	7
8	9	10	11	12	13	14
15	16	17	18	19	20	21
22	23	24	25	26	27	28
29	30	31				

May 2015

Su	Mo	Tu	We	Th	Fr	Sa
					1	2
3	4	5	6	7	8	9
10	11	12	13	14	15	16
17	18	19	20	21	22	23
24	25	26	27	28	29	30
31						

Pastel Globes

The frosts have come and gone.
Spring is heading towards summer.
Tender grapevines have awakened.
Tiny flower clusters magically appear.
Insects lovingly pollinate each one.

Petals dry and blow away.
Pastel globes begin to slowly swell.
Pale green leaves protect her progeny from
Wind that easily tears clusters asunder, or
Birds that feast heartily on young grapes.

In each orb lies the future.
The promise of their kind is hidden within.
A young seed waits his turn to grow.
Come fall, if all is right, to the soil he'll drop.
Next spring, perhaps a new vine will eagerly sprout.

- Dawn L. Huffaker

Photo by Marilyn Huffaker

May 2015

Sunday	Monday	Tuesday	Wednesday	Thursday	Friday	Saturday
					1	2
3	4	5	6	7	8	9
10	11	12	13	14	15	16
Mother's Day 17	18	19	20	21	22	23
24	Memorial Day 25	26	27	28	29	30
31						

April 2015

Su	Mo	Tu	We	Th	Fr	Sa
			1	2	3	4
5	6	7	8	9	10	11
12	13	14	15	16	17	18
19	20	21	22	23	24	25
26	27	28	29	30		

June 2015

Su	Mo	Tu	We	Th	Fr	Sa
	1	2	3	4	5	6
7	8	9	10	11	12	13
14	15	16	17	18	19	20
21	22	23	24	25	26	27
28	29	30				

Daylilies

Summer's sun stretches down.
Waves of heat waft off of every surface.
Daylilies bask in the intense, June warmth.
Tangerine flowers turn towards this light
Gathering all that it has to offer
Like baby birds in a nest.

Daylilies delight in being
The center of attention.
Their burnished faces beam with pride.
They seem to say, "Look at us.
Aren't we the prettiest?
Aren't we the best that God ever made?"

Give them their due. They are quite special.
Seek out a daylily and silently converse.
Let one teach you about breathless beauty.
Let another teach you about fearless faith.
They trust God for each summer day to return
Resting beneath while icy winter reigns.

- Dawn L. Huffaker

June 2015

Sunday	Monday	Tuesday	Wednesday	Thursday	Friday	Saturday
31	1	2	3	4	5	6
7	8	9	10	11	12	13
14	15	16	17	18	19	20
21	22	23	24	25	26	27
Summer Solstice **16:38 UTC** Father's Day	29	30	1	2	3	4

Flag Day (under 14)

Beaming Dianthus

July has arrived with much fanfare.
America celebrates her freedom.
Summer monsoon storms punctuate
The hot afternoons bringing relief.
Dianthus have burst from their buds
Looking eagerly towards the sky.

Beaming Dianthus
Dream of the distant heavens
Where they would rather
Be streaking across the night sky
Like fireworks quickly gaining altitude-
Glowing with such tangible delight.

For you see, a long time ago,
Dianthus flowers were once meteorites
That fell to earth when they came too close.
Gravity pulled them nearer and nearer.
Atmosphere shattered them to dust-
Which then sprouted the following spring.

Ruffled petals grace them.
Shiny stamens surround tiny faces.
Ancient intellect shows from deep within.
Ambassadors from beyond our world
Who continue to spread magical delight
To those who cherish them in gardens fair.

– Dawn L. Huffaker

July 2015

Sunday	Monday	Tuesday	Wednesday	Thursday	Friday	Saturday
28	29	30	1 ●	2	3	4 Independence Day
5	6	7	8 ●	9	10	11
12	13	14	15 ●	16	17	18
19	20	21	22	23 ●	24	25
26	27	28	29	30	31 ●	1

Photo by Marilyn Huffaker

Cheery Cosmos

On tall, shaggy, green stems
Bloom the happiest of blossoms.
Never a sad day where they live.
Nothing can make them blue.

Cheery Cosmos bob gently on the breeze.
Every bounce makes them giggle.
They can't help but laugh.
The wind tickles them so.

Join them out in the garden.
Learn to let go and relax.
See the beauty all around.
Become childlike and gentle like them.

Cosmos nod to each other.
They nod their heads to you.
These flowers celebrate the moment.
What a beautiful time to be alive, indeed!

– Dawn L. Huffaker

August 2015

Sunday	Monday	Tuesday	Wednesday	Thursday	Friday	Saturday
26	27	28	29	30	31	1
2	3	4	5	6	7	8
9	10	11	12	13	14	15
16	17	18	19	20	21	22
23	24	25	26	27	28	29
30	31	1	2	3		

July 2015

Su	Mo	Tu	We	Th	Fr	Sa
			1	2	3	4
5	6	7	8	9	10	11
12	13	14	15	16	17	18
19	20	21	22	23	24	25
26	27	28	29	30	31	

September 2015

Su	Mo	Tu	We	Th	Fr	Sa
		1	2	3	4	5
6	7	8	9	10	11	12
13	14	15	16	17	18	19
20	21	22	23	24	25	26
27	28	29	30			

Gentle Friend

Mule deer buck quietly crosses the meadow.
He savors a mouthful of late summer grass.
It is the best of the year-flavorful and sweet.
Gentle deer pauses to nibble a tender morsel.

Noise from the house catches his attention.
Looking to see who is there, interrupts his feast.
The buck poses with such ease of grace.
Camera catches this magical moment.

Gentle friend you are to us who live here.
We are humbled by your presence.
You bless us with your dignity and refinement.
Our lives are made better because of you.

- Dawn L. Huffaker

Photo by Ron Huffaker

September 2015

Sunday	Monday	Tuesday	Wednesday	Thursday	Friday	Saturday
30	31	1	2	3	4	5 ◐
6	7 Labor Day	8	9	10	11	12
13 ●	14	15	16	17	18	19
20	21 ◐	22	23 **Autumnal Equinox** **08:20 UTC**	24	25	26
27 ●	28	29	30	1	2	3

August 2015							October 2015						
Su	Mo	Tu	We	Th	Fr	Sa	Su	Mo	Tu	We	Th	Fr	Sa
						1					1	2	3
2	3	4	5	6	7	8	4	5	6	7	8	9	10
9	10	11	12	13	14	15	11	12	13	14	15	16	17
16	17	18	19	20	21	22	18	19	20	21	22	23	24
23	24	25	26	27	28	29	25	26	27	28	29	30	31
30	31												

Sleepy Mimosa

Sleepy Mimosa yawns and sighs.
He greets the morning sun through
Half-open eyes which feel so very tired.

Sweet memories of the summer
Play through the recesses of his mind.
Where had the time of plenty gone?

Wind comes by to say, "Good morning!"
The movement makes his leaves
Rustle and turn loose to waft to ground.

Fog of sleep briefly lifts from him.
Startled by the dropping leaves,
Sleepy Mimosa spies his golden foliage.

With pride, he glistens in the sun.
Soon he will sleep through the winter months.
Dreams of summer will keep him warm.

- Dawn L. Huffaker

October 2015

Sunday	Monday	Tuesday	Wednesday	Thursday	Friday	Saturday
27	28	29	30	1	2	3
4	5	6	7	8	9	10
11	12 Columbus Day	13	14	15	16	17
18	19	20	21	22	23	24
25	26	27	28	29	30	31 Halloween

September 2015

Su	Mo	Tu	We	Th	Fr	Sa
		1	2	3	4	5
6	7	8	9	10	11	12
13	14	15	16	17	18	19
20	21	22	23	24	25	26
27	28	29	30			

November 2015

Su	Mo	Tu	We	Th	Fr	Sa
1	2	3	4	5	6	7
8	9	10	11	12	13	14
15	16	17	18	19	20	21
22	23	24	25	26	27	28
29	30					

Still-life

Fall turns to winter
Overnight.
Snow rimes the trees
Hoary white.
Ground is muffled with
Downy stillness.

Sunlight sparkles
Off cold diamond crystals.
Lingering fog slides
Between nodding branches.
Sky watches mesmerized
This beauty below.

What once was
Is fast asleep.
Clocks have slowed
To a crawl.
Nature has become
A still-life.

- Dawn L. Huffaker

November 2015

Sunday	Monday	Tuesday	Wednesday	Thursday	Friday	Saturday
1 Daylight savings time ends	2	3	4	5	6	7
8	9	10	11 Veteran's Day	12	13	14
15	16	17	18	19	20	21
22	23	24	25 Thanksgiving	26	27	28
29	30					

God's Gift

Morning breaks
Cold and clear.
Sunshine flows
Over the eastern horizon
To illuminate
The new-fallen snow.

Like powdered sugar
It softly coats
The forest's trees
With a hint
Of what is to come
From the afternoon storm.

Clock starts ticking
Towards tonight-
Christmas Eve.
A very white Christmas
Will be God's gift to
To celebrate Jesus's birth.

Have a Merry Christmas!

- Dawn L. Huffaker

Photo by Chris Knight

December 2015

Sunday	Monday	Tuesday	Wednesday	Thursday	Friday	Saturday
29	30	1	2	3 ◐	4	5
6	7	8	9	10	11 ●	12
13	14	15	16	17	18 ◑	19
20	21	22 Winter Solstice 04:48 UTC	23	24 Christmas Eve	25 ○ Christmas Day	26
27	28	29	30	31 New Year's Eve	1	2
3	4	5	6	7		

Notes

2016

January
S	M	T	W	T	F	S
					1	2
3	4	5	6	7	8	9
10	11	12	13	14	15	16
17	18	19	20	21	22	23
24	25	26	27	28	29	30
31						

February
S	M	T	W	T	F	S
	1	2	3	4	5	6
7	8	9	10	11	12	13
14	15	16	17	18	19	20
21	22	23	24	25	26	27
28	29					

March
S	M	T	W	T	F	S
		1	2	3	4	5
6	7	8	9	10	11	12
13	14	15	16	17	18	19
20	21	22	23	24	25	26
27	28	29	30	31		

April
S	M	T	W	T	F	S
					1	2
3	4	5	6	7	8	9
10	11	12	13	14	15	16
17	18	19	20	21	22	23
24	25	26	27	28	29	30

May
S	M	T	W	T	F	S
1	2	3	4	5	6	7
8	9	10	11	12	13	14
15	16	17	18	19	20	21
22	23	24	25	26	27	28
29	30	31				

June
S	M	T	W	T	F	S
			1	2	3	4
5	6	7	8	9	10	11
12	13	14	15	16	17	18
19	20	21	22	23	24	25
26	27	28	29	30		

July
S	M	T	W	T	F	S
					1	2
3	4	5	6	7	8	9
10	11	12	13	14	15	16
17	18	19	20	21	22	23
24	25	26	27	28	29	30
31						

August
S	M	T	W	T	F	S
	1	2	3	4	5	6
7	8	9	10	11	12	13
14	15	16	17	18	19	20
21	22	23	24	25	26	27
28	29	30	31			

September
S	M	T	W	T	F	S
				1	2	3
4	5	6	7	8	9	10
11	12	13	14	15	16	17
18	19	20	21	22	23	24
25	26	27	28	29	30	

October
S	M	T	W	T	F	S
						1
2	3	4	5	6	7	8
9	10	11	12	13	14	15
16	17	18	19	20	21	22
23	24	25	26	27	28	29
30	31					

November
S	M	T	W	T	F	S
		1	2	3	4	5
6	7	8	9	10	11	12
13	14	15	16	17	18	19
20	21	22	23	24	25	26
27	28	29	30			

December
S	M	T	W	T	F	S
				1	2	3
4	5	6	7	8	9	10
11	12	13	14	15	16	17
18	19	20	21	22	23	24
25	26	27	28	29	30	31

www.ingramcontent.com/pod-product-compliance
Lightning Source LLC
Chambersburg PA
CBHW060821290526
45792CB00005BB/1744